Library of Congress Number: 73-10388   ISBN: O-87191-261-1

Published by Creative Education, Mankato, Minnesota 56001
Prepared for the Publisher by Educreative Systems, Inc.
Distributed by Childrens Press, 1224 West Van Buren Street, Chicago, Illinois 60607

Library of Congress Cataloging in Publication Data
Olsen, James T.
James T. Olsen.
   Joe Namath: the king of football.
   SUMMARY: A biography of the football player who rose to fame as quarterback of the New York Jets.
   1. Namath, Joe Willie, 1943-   Juvenile literature. [1. Namath, Joe Willie, 1943-
   2. Football—Biography] I. Title. GV939.N28E38 796.33'2'094 [B] [92] 73-10388
ISBN 0-871,91-265-1
3 Sports- Biography

JOE NAMATH

THE KING OF FOOTBALL

By James T. Olsen

Illustrated by Montie Salmela

"Yeah, Joe Willie!"

"Did you see that ball? It went right over the telephone wires!"

"Sure wish my kid brother could throw a football like that."

The "kid" was the brother of John, Bobby and Franklin Namath. His name was Joseph William Namath and he was born on May 13, 1943, in Beaver Falls, Pennsylvania. When he was five his brothers needed a quarterback for their front yard football games. Joe was it. All the boys agreed that Joe shouldn't be tackled. Since Joe was always in the open he developed a great throwing arm. By the age of six he could hit the stump of a tree from 40 yards, or throw a ball out of sight or over the telephone lines.

The Namath family lived "on the wrong side of the tracks" in Beaver Falls, a steel mill town about 28 miles from Pittsburgh. Joe's father, Frank Namath, was a steel mill worker in that town.

Even though Joe lived in a poor section of town, he found his life in Beaver Falls exciting. Joe and his friends had really good times. As Joe said years later, "In back of our house was the Fame Laundry and we put so many footballs, baseballs and stones through the windows that they finally covered them over with wallboard. Half a block down the street was a bottling plant and then a junkyard, and we'd pick up the junk at the river and sell it at the junkyard, except some of the guys would borrow from the back of the junkyard and sell it again at the front. Then there was the ice company to fool around in and the river to swim in and the railroad tracks. We could get the rocks from the railroad tracks for our gang fights . . . . It was just great growing up there." Joe's boyhood wasn't all play. Joe helped his family by earning money. He shined shoes. He ran errands, and he worked as a golf caddy.

When Joe entered Beaver Falls High School, he was a star athlete. He starred in football, baseball, and basketball. He had a C plus average in his studies. Joe loved high school because he was the star. But football was his favorite sport. Joe remembers, "We had a great coach and I'll be talking about that team as long as I live. In my senior year, I completed eighty four out of one hundred and twenty passes and not one time did I get tackled behind the line. That was the blocking I had."

When Joe entered his fourth year of high school, he had many offers. Fifty two colleges and universities wanted Joe to play at their schools. There were also offers from six major league baseball teams. Joe decided not to pass up the chance to go to college. He wanted to go to the University of Maryland, but his grades weren't good enough. So he tried the University of Alabama instead. He was accepted there and enrolled in that school in the summer of 1961.

Joe's choice of Alabama was a good one because Alabama had one of the finest football coaches in the United States, Paul "Bear" Bryant. Joe remembers the first time he met Bryant. He was late reporting for training, but Coach Bryant had nothing bad to say to him. Joe was invited up to the tower where the Coach watched the team work out. "Coach Bryant hollered down to me 'C'mon up' . . . I think Coach Bryant talked to me for about thirty minutes and that was the first time I ran across a Southern accent . . . I just believe he is not only a great coach but a great man." Bryant's attitude toward Namath was very simple. As he put it: "Joe Namath was the greatest athlete I ever coached."

Joe's athletic record at the University of Alabama was even better than his record in high school. Everyone could see Joe was a great athlete and an even better football player. In his second year at Alabama, Joe was the starting quarterback. He led his team to a record of ten wins out of eleven games. In that year, for example, Joe completed seventy-six out of one hundred and forty-six passes. In his third year, Joe completed sixty-three passes in one hundred and twenty eight tries. But near the end of that season, Joe Namath was suddenly dropped from the football squad because he had been keeping late hours. A curfew was one of the training rules that Coach Bryant had laid down at the very beginning. As a result, Joe missed the last game of the regular football season. He also lost his chance to play in the post-season Sugar Bowl game.

Joe learned an important lesson. Coach Bryant would treat him just like any other Alabama football player. Not long after this happened Alabama's center, Galen McCullough, said, "Joe was a real leader . . . for the first time. Before, he used to just do his job and expect everyone else to do theirs. But now he was always after everybody to do better."

Joe loved football, but it's a tough game. During one game he stopped short in a play. Because he came to such a quick stop his right knee gave out. A few weeks later in a game against Florida, Joe Namath's knee collapsed again. Several months later, in December, he suffered a third injury to his knee while he was practicing for the New Year's Day Orange Bowl game. Alabama played against Texas and Joe had to sit the game out. He was benched because of his injury. At halftime, Alabama was behind and Coach Bryant decided to risk sending Joe in to play. Joe limped out onto the field. He played his best even though his knee hurt. His best was not good enough. The final score was Texas - 21, Alabama - 17.

Joe Namath's days as a college star were at an end. He was ready to play pro ball. The question was: which team would he choose? Joe's answer was simple: the team that would pay him the most money. The two teams that wanted Joe the most were the New York Jets of the American Football League (AFL) and the Saint Louis Cardinals of the National Football League (NFL). Each team tried to outbid the other. Joe then hired Mike Bite, a lawyer from Birmingham, Alabama. Mike Bite was to represent Joe and handle the bidding of the two teams. On January 2, 1965, Joe Namath signed with the Jets. His contract was to

be for three years. His fee was $387,000 and a Lincoln convertible. Joe dropped out of college. His "football" education was over. He was ready to start work.

When Joe arrived to play with the Jets, the Jets' coach, Weeb Ewbank, decided that "Namath was the best prospect since Sammy Baugh." (Sammy Baugh was the famed quarterback of the Washington Redskins. Many people thought Sammy was one of the greatest football players who ever lived.) Ewbank also liked the way Joe thought about the game of football. Ewbank said that Namath didn't know about losing. He only understood winning.

Since Joe was the highest paid rookie in the history of sports, he had to give the Jets all he had. His future was at stake. But Joe was cool about the whole thing. The way he put it was: "Man, I'm tired of hearing about it. You want to know the truth? If I didn't have Mike Bite and some other good people around me, I'd have signed for almost anything. I just want to play football, and I'm just lucky I got all that money, too." Coach Ewbank put it all very simply when he said, "From now on, it depends on how the kid produces. If he doesn't, we'll be the laughing stock of sports."

Joe didn't plan to be anybody's laughing stock. The first day that Joe showed up for practice with the Jets, Coach Ewbank watched him throw the ball. He told him, "Joe, you're throwing off your back foot and you're not getting enough follow-through." "Don't worry, Coach. Once I get loosened up, I'll hit all those guys."

Joe found those early months hard. His high salary, the way he dressed, and the way he often spoke his mind often caused trouble for him. One of his teammates didn't like his long, dark hair and flowing mustache. That didn't bother Joe. He said: "The greatest guy in the world wore long hair and a beard."

After the Jets won the AFL championship, Joe asked for cases of champagne. He wanted them opened in the locker room after the game was over. The players were not supposed to drink anything alcoholic in the dressing room. The President of the AFL objected to Joe's champagne idea. That didn't stop Joe. "Mr. Woodward tried to tell me that it was bad for the image of football, that it was bad for the kids to see it. But the real image of football is brutality—why don't they tell the kids like it is?"

That's the kind of honesty you expect from Joe Namath. He has always let people know what's on his mind. So he was ready for the tests that his Jet teammates laid on him. As one of the Jets put it when

Joe first joined the Jets: "They're gonna test him. I think first they'll try to get at him mentally, giving him a hard time and trying to get him to run around and desert his game plan. I think they're gonna try to intimidate him."

It would take some doing to intimidate Joe Namath, to make him unsure of himself. Joe had been one of the few white kids to grow up in a neighborhood that was almost all black. His best friends were black; his high school basketball team was all black. Then

Joe went to the University of Alabama. He was with all whites for the first time in his life. He would have debates with his classmates and with his teammates about black people. Joe Namath recalls that he "used to get into debates and one of his nicknames was 'Nigger'. I came to understand that. They were raised a different way than I was, so I didn't try to tell them how to live." But Joe didn't change the way he lived either. He just saw things very differently. The neighborhood that Joe grew up in didn't have the prejudices that many southern neighborhoods had. Joe didn't grow up with the prejudices that some of his southern schoolmates had grown up with.

"My best friend that I was raised with was Linwood Alford and he's colored and he was on our basketball team. Now he works in a steel mill and part-time in a clothing store, but he lived across the street and I used to sleep in his house and he used to sleep in mine. We had this basket that we fixed to a backboard and fastened to a two-by-four, and we used to carry that around and tie it to a light pole so we could play at night. We'd play out there when it was so cold we had to wear ear muffs and mittens, and when it was raining or snowing we'd go down to my cellar and practice dribbling."

"The thing about Linwood was that he'd get so tied up in a game he'd cry. But I wanted to win, too, so I wouldn't lay down and he'd be crying and saying: 'Let's play some more.' Linwood's dad died when we were both very young and his mother had to raise seven kids and she was a lovely lady. She was down-to-earth and honest. When she spoke she spoke softly and all the kids listened. They listened because she used to sit on the porch with a switch and a pile of stones, and when Linwood and his brother, David, would get to fighting, she'd throw rocks at 'em."

"I remember when we were very small and my dad was going to work at the mill and he kissed me goodbye. Linwood was standing there and he said, 'What about me?' So my dad kissed Linwood goodbye, too. Then I remember when we were about ten, we went into this pizza place and we tried to buy a pizza and the woman looked at Linwood and said, 'You get out of here.' That was the first time I ran into prejudice." Joe didn't like prejudice then, and he certainly doesn't like it now.

That's the kind of man Joe Namath is. Another example of his knowing his own mind goes something like this: One night shortly after he had signed with the Jets, he was in an expensive restaurant with two of his friends. The waiter had very definite ideas about what Joe and his friends should eat.

"Now you start with the clams oregano," the waiter said, "and then the special homemade noodles with the special sauce and then maybe the veal rollatine or . . ."

"I'll have spaghetti and meatballs," Joe said.

"What! the waiter said. He looked at Joe as if he were crazy. "You mean you came to a restaurant like this to get spaghetti and meatballs? That you can get anyplace you want."

"Spaghetti and meatballs," Joe said softly.

"So," the waiter went on, "you will start with . . ." Joe looked the waiter in the eye. He said very softly, "Spaghetti and meatballs."

And that's what Joe got. He was used to getting

his own way both in restaurants and on the football field. When Joe was playing for Beaver Falls High School, a teammate tried to call a play for Joe in a tough game. Joe told him to shut up. The teammate kept on. Joe walked over to the coach and whispered something into the coach's ear. The coach came over to the players and told Joe's teammate: "Get out!"

Joe thinks about football a great deal. His easy going ways hide his seriousness about football. One night at a party, a friend asked Joe what he was thinking about. Over the blare of the rock music, Joe answered: "I'm thinking that if I can just get a good flight on the ball early in the season I can have a good year. There's something else I'd like to do, too, and that's to play a perfect game. I've never done that and that's what I'm driving for."

After Joe Namath joined the Jets, everyone knew that he would be the starting quarterback for the team. But at the beginning of the 1965 season, Joe found himself on the bench. Coach Ewbank worked him into the lineup gradually and by the middle of the season Namath was the first-string quarterback. By the end of the season, it was clear that Joe Namath was going to be one of the football greats. The Jets finished in second place in the Eastern Division that season. But one of Joe's greatest moments happened in the January

1966 All-Star game at Houston.

At the beginning of the second half, the All-Stars were trailing the Buffalo Bills by a score of 13 to 6. Namath was sent in and passed for two touchdowns. This gave the Stars a 30 to 19 victory. Namath played this game, as well as many others, with a great deal of pain. He is always troubled by badly injured knees. His knee operations occur at the rate of about one a

year. But no matter what the doctors do, Joe says that the pain is sometimes more terrible than could be imagined.

Joe Namath also knows that on any play a blind side block could finish him forever. As one coach puts it: "He has tremendous courage." Joe doesn't use words like courage nor does he talk very much about the constant pain in his knees. All he tries to do is be as good as he can be. It is not easy for Joe because if one of the huge players from the other team was to break through the line they would do their best to break Joe's ribs, step on his hands, snap his knees or break his neck. They would like to stop Namath once and for all.

Joe has to watch out. A lot of players are bigger than he is. Along with the knee pain and the danger his body is in, Joe has to keep his head. He must not only be able to throw a football 30 to 50 yards and never miss his mark, but he must rule his teammates with his thinking. He must plan out—figure ahead. And he must also give his teammates spirit, hope, and the feeling that they are going to win.

Out on the field Joe thinks hard and plays hard, in spite of the pain. This may be the reason that once off the field Namath lives a fast and hard life. He likes to party and have a roaring good time. He also likes the theater and has even been on TV and made a movie. People teased him by calling him "Broadway Joe."

This party boy is the same man who does exercises every day, even though the pain in his knees is terrible. The doctor who did the first of his three knee operations asked him to begin exercising his leg right after he awoke from the operation. He did. And he does the same exercises today to make his knees stronger.

Joe Namath says it best: "It was a lot tougher than I figured." It was tough but Joe stuck it out.

There are many reasons for Broadway Joe's success. He is a good-looking man who has a quick smile. He has an easy way with people. The charm helped end some of the problems between him and other football players, especially the Jet players. Joe is aware of his good looks and easy-going personality. As he says about himself: "Ah can't wait until tomorrow because I get better looking every day."

He may be getting better looking, but he is also getting older. His lawyer, Mike Bite, is still investing Joe's money in many businesses. Joe only takes $25,000

a year for his own use and all of the rest of the money is handled by Mike Bite. During the football season, Joe used to share a penthouse apartment in New York's upper east side. He had two roommates: Joe Abruzzese and a sportswriter by the name of Joe Hirsch. During the offseason he goes to Beaver Falls and stays with his mother and stepfather. He now has a fancy apartment of his own.

Football is Joe Namath's life even when he is taking it easy at home, in New York or in Beaver Falls.

He has carefully worked at becoming a good football player. Linebacker Larry Grantham said: "Sure Joe has grown up a lot but we all do. A football player comes out of college into the pros, and he's one of about 1,100 people doing what he does. If you're a starting quarterback, then you are only one of twenty-six. It takes everybody a while to get his feet on the ground. I don't see how he handled it as well as he did."

Don Maynard, who has caught Joe's passes for

eight years always tells people there is an easy way to get a true picture of Joe. ". . . Read about Joe's football and multiply; read about his night life and divide."

And here is Coach Ewbank: "I never had any trouble with Joe. I don't care anything about his night life, but he has always been a serious football player, willing to do anything to help the team. He'll take a movie projector home and study game movies for two, three hours a night, I guess. He plays with pain and never moans about it. And he hasn't changed."

Joe Namath has also helped change other football players as well. This is shown by the words of Guard Dave Herman. "It isn't Joe who has changed. It is the world who has changed toward Joe—or caught up with him. He used to be one of the only players with long hair, for example. But now, he's one of the few players without a mustache."

Joe is an athlete who does his best in every one of his games. He has a lot of nerve because he holds the ball a long time before he finally throws it. Many quarterbacks throw the ball too soon, but Joe never does. He always waits until the very last second—that last split second—until the rushing players are almost on top of him. Then he throws the ball with perfect aim. And then he gets hit in the mouth. But he throws without thinking about getting hit in the mouth.

Namath can also lead a team. He can make his teammates play better than they think they can. He is the leader on the field. He comes onto the field sure of what he wants done and then he sees to it that the team does it. The coach doesn't often bother to send plays into Namath. If he does, then it is understood that Joe doesn't have to follow them. Joe Namath likes to work on his own and then tell the team what he wants them to do. Namath has done very well playing the game this way. Joe and his receivers work so well together that the receivers never look back. The passing is so well organized that the receiver runs his pattern. When he does look back for a quick moment, there is the ball.

While Joe Namath may have never graduated from the University of Alabama, his football playing

shows a man who can think, carry out and lead. Add
this to his quickness and co-ordination and you have
a player who "gets rid of the ball so fast you can't
rush him. And follows through all the way, like any
quarterback who ever played for 'Bear' Bryant." His

teammates have complete faith in him and that is part of the reason the Jets have been winners even when the odds were against them.

There are those who say that Joe Namath has made over the world of professional football. He is devoted to the game and his job. But as he sees it, his life off the ball field is his own business. Joe puts it very well when he says: "I believe in letting a guy live the way he wants to if he doesn't hurt anyone. I feel that everything I do is O.K. for me and does not affect anyone else. Look man, I live and let live. I like everybody."

As Joe sees it, he has always been a winner from the time he was six years old and playing Little League Baseball. That's the way it has been for Joe and if he has anything to do with it, that's the way it'll always be. Joe Willie—Broadway Joe—he's the king of football.

JACKIE ROBINSON
MUHAMMAD ALI
O. J. SIMPSON
JOHNNY BENCH
WILT CHAMBERLAIN
ARNOLD PALMER
A. J. FOYT
JOHNNY UNITAS
GORDIE HOWE
WALT FRAZIER
PHIL AND TONY ESPOSITO
BOB GRIESE

JACK NICKLAUS
BILL RUSSELL
MARK SPITZ
VINCE LOMBARDI
BILLIE JEAN KING
ROBERTO CLEMENTE
JOE NAMATH
BOBBY HULL
HANK AARON
JERRY WEST
TOM SEAVER

superstars! superstars! superstars!

CREATIVE EDUCATION SPORTS SUPERSTARS

FRANK ROBINSON
PANCHO GONZALES
LEE TREVINO
KAREEM ABDUL JABBAR
JEAN CLAUDE KILLY
EVONNE GOOLAGONG
ARTHUR ASHE
SECRETARIAT
ROGER STAUBACH
FRAN TARKENTON
BOBBY ORR
LARRY CSONKA
JOHNNY MILLER
FRANCO HARRIS

BILL WALTON
ALAN PAGE
PEGGY FLEMING
OLGA KORBUT
DON SCHULA
MICKEY MANTLE
EVEL KNIEVEL
JIMMY CONNORS
CHRIS EVERT
PETER REVSON
KATHY WHITWORTH
JACKIE STEWART
STAN SMITH
JANET LYNN